# KINDERGARTEN
## Activity Book
### Zoo Animals

# KINDERGARTEN
## Activity Book
### Zoo Animals

75 Games to Practice Early Reading,
Writing, and Math Skills

**Lauren Thompson**

ILLUSTRATED BY
**Jennie Bradley**

callisto
publishing
an imprint of Sourcebooks

Copyright © 2022 by Callisto Publishing LLC
Cover and internal design © 2022 by Callisto Publishing LLC
Illustrations © Jennie Bradley, 2021
Series Designer: John Calmeyer
Interior and Cover Designer: Tricia Jang
Art Producer: Janice Ackerman
Editor: Julie Haverkate
Production Editor: Ashley Polikoff
Production Manager: Holly Haydash

Callisto Kids and the colophon are registered trademarks of Callisto Publishing LLC.

All rights reserved. No part of this book may be reproduced in any form or by any electronic or mechanical means including information storage and retrieval systems—except in the case of brief quotations embodied in critical articles or reviews—without permission in writing from its publisher, Sourcebooks LLC.

All brand names and product names used in this book are trademarks, registered trademarks, or trade names of their respective holders. Callisto Publishing is not associated with any product or vendor in this book.

Published by Callisto Publishing LLC C/O Sourcebooks LLC
P.O. Box 4410, Naperville, Illinois 60567-4410
(630) 961-3900
callistopublishing.com

This product conforms to all applicable CPSC and CPSIA standards.

Source of Production: 1010 Printing Asia Limited, Kwun Tong, Hong Kong, China
Date of Production: June 2024
Run Number: 5042130

Printed and bound in China
OGP 2

# CONTENTS

# ANSWER KEY

# NOTE TO CAREGIVERS

Are you ready for a fun trip to the zoo? This book is packed with 75 zoo animal–themed games and activities to reinforce skills that children are learning in kindergarten. It is the perfect size to keep at home or to bring along for some screen-free entertainment on the go!

As a teacher and mother of five, I know how important it is to provide opportunities for children to lay strong foundations in reading and math. I have a degree in early elementary education and experience as a classroom teacher as well as a homeschool mom. I have been writing curricula and creating resources for parents and teachers since 2012.

In this book, your child will complete dot to dots, mazes, color by numbers, picture hunts, and more! Designed to grab and hold a child's attention, these engaging activities also incorporate reading and math skills such as letters, sounds, rhyming, blends, sight words, numbers, skip counting, comparing, and basic addition and subtraction. The activities are divided up and color coded by concept, and each section progresses from easiest to hardest, allowing your child to build confidence as they go.

Children love to play, and with these colorful games and activities, they may not even realize they are practicing essential reading and math skills! At first, you may need to help your child with the directions, but once they become familiar with the activities, they can work more independently.

Enjoy watching your child learn, and have a great visit to the zoo!

—Lauren

# Animal Alphabet

Say and trace each letter.

# Awesome Anteater

Trace and write.

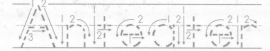

Follow the path with the letter A to help
the anteater find the anthill.

# Busy Bears

Trace and write.

Bear

Find and circle the B's and b's hidden
by this bear-y cute family.

# Clever Crocodile

Trace and write.

Crocodile

What begins with the letter C?
Color the crocodiles with objects that begin with C green.

# Darling Ducks

Trace and write.

The ducks are stuck! Circle the upper or lowercase
letter that comes next in the pattern.

# Enormous Elephant

Trace and write.

Use the key to spot the world's
largest land mammal!

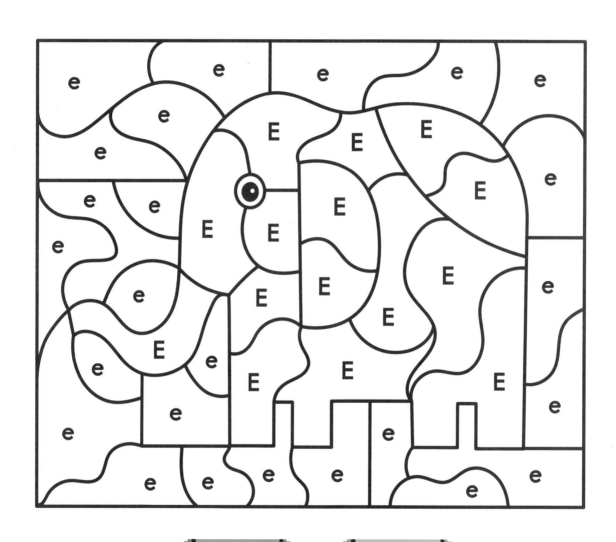

# Funny Fox

Trace and write.

The foxes are on the hunt! Help them find and circle the hidden pictures that begin with F using the key below.

# Graceful Gorilla

## Trace and write.

It's snack time! Help the gorilla by tracing the circles and coloring the grapes.

# Happy Hippo

Trace and write.

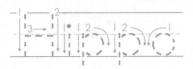

Follow the path of objects that begin with H to help the hippo get to the water hole.

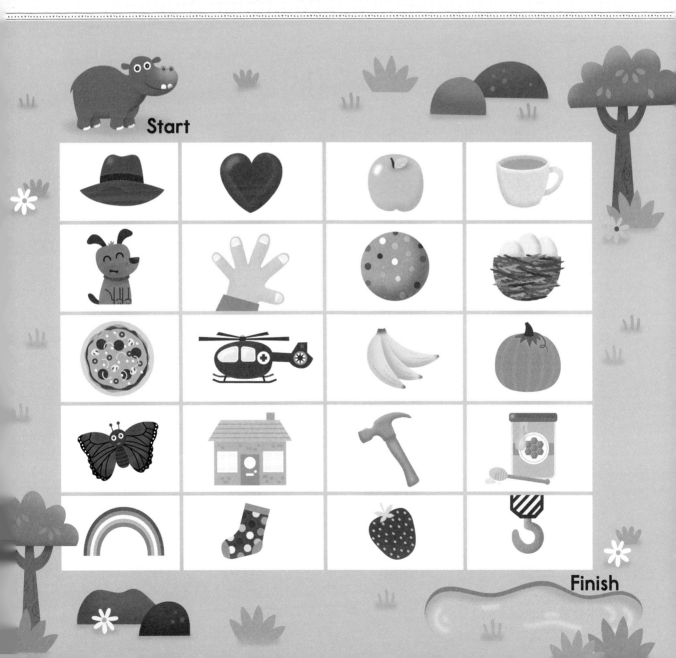

# Intelligent Impala

Trace and write.

Connect the lowercase i's and uppercase I's
to make this African antelope.

# Joyful Jellyfish

Trace and write.

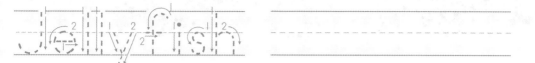

Look out for jellyfish! Color objects beginning with
the letter J **pink**. Use any color for the rest.

# Kind Kangaroo

Trace and write.

Kangaroo _____

The joey lost its mama! Follow the letters
K and k to help the joey find her.

# Lucky Lion

Trace and write.

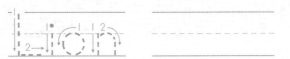

While the lions are relaxing in their habitat,
find and circle the hidden L's.

# Marvelous Meerkat

Trace and write.

Use the color key to help the meerkats
reveal the hidden letter.

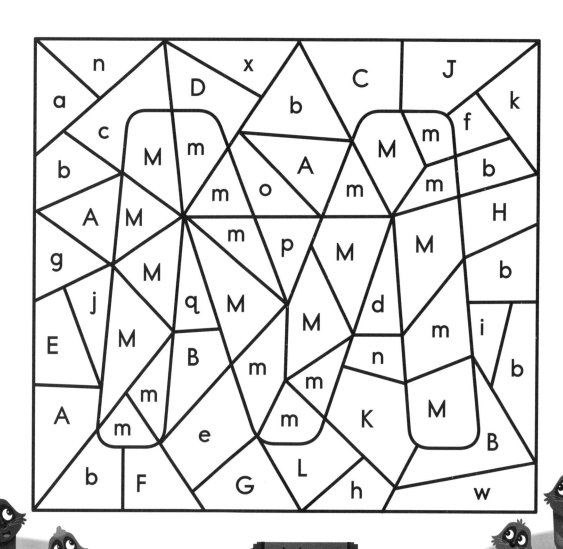

# Nifty Narwhal

Trace and write.

Color in the bubbles of things that begin with N.
Cross out things that do NOT begin with N.

# Obedient Owl

Trace and write.

"Owl" bet you can circle which letter comes next in the pattern!

# Pretty Peacock

Trace and write.

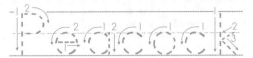

Strut your stuff! Draw a line to match
each picture to the letter it starts with.

# Quiet Quail

Trace and write.

Connect the lowercase q's and uppercase Q's
to make this quiet game bird.

# Rad Rhino

Trace and write.

These rhinos have poor eyesight! Help them find and circle the hidden pictures that begin with R using the key below.

# Silly Sloth

Trace and write.

Sloth _____

Follow the pictures that begin with S
to help the slow sloth climb to the tree.

Finish

Start

# Terrific Tiger

Trace and write.

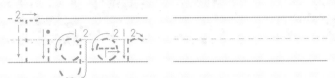

Use the color key to reveal the largest living cat in the world!

| G | G | G | t | G | G | t | G | G | G |
|---|---|---|---|---|---|---|---|---|---|
| G | G | t | t | T | T | t | t | G | G |
| G | G | t | t | t | t | t | t | G | G |
| G | T | T | j | t | t | r | T | T | G |
| G | t | t | ● | t | t | ● | t | t | G |
| G | T | T | t | t | t | t | T | T | G |
| G | t | t | s | P | P | f | t | t | G |
| G | T | T | n | u | a | x | T | T | G |
| G | G | t | b | m | q | e | t | G | G |
| G | G | G | t | t | t | t | G | G | G |

| t | T | P | G |
|---|---|---|---|

# Unique Umbrellabird

Trace and write.

Umbrellabird

Connect the letters from A to U of the alphabet to make an umbrellabird. This unusual bird lives in the rain forest.

# Vocal Vulture

Trace and write.

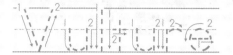

Find and circle the hidden
V's and v's in the picture.

**How many did you find?** _____

# Wise Whale

Trace and write.

Circle the whales with objects beginning with W.
Cross out the rest.

# Extraordinary X-Ray Fish

Trace and write.

_____

_____

Use the key to color the letters and find the X-ray fish.
Can you spot their skeletons?

| Y | Y | Y | Y | Y | Y | Y | Y | Y | Y | Y | Y |
|---|---|---|---|---|---|---|---|---|---|---|---|
| Y | Y | Y | Y | Y | w | w | Y | Y | Y | Y | Y |
| Y | x | Y | Y | Y | Y | W | W | Y | Y | Y | Y |
| Y | x | x | Y | Y | Y | Y | y | y | Y | Y | Y |
| Y | Y | x | x | Y | X | X | X | X | X | Y | Y |
| Y | Y | x | X | X | X | X | X | X | W | X | Y |
| Y | Y | x | X | X | X | X | X | X | X | X | Y |
| Y | Y | x | x | Y | X | X | X | X | X | Y | Y |
| Y | x | x | Y | Y | Y | Y | y | y | Y | Y | Y |
| Y | x | Y | Y | Y | Y | W | W | Y | Y | Y | Y |
| Y | Y | Y | Y | Y | w | w | Y | Y | Y | Y | Y |
| Y | Y | Y | Y | Y | Y | Y | Y | Y | Y | Y | Y |
| Y | Y | Y | Y | Y | Y | Y | Y | Y | Y | Y | Y |

| x | w | y |
|---|---|---|
| X | W | Y |

# Young Yak

Trace and write.

These cow cousins are looking for a pattern! Help them by circling the object that completes the pattern.

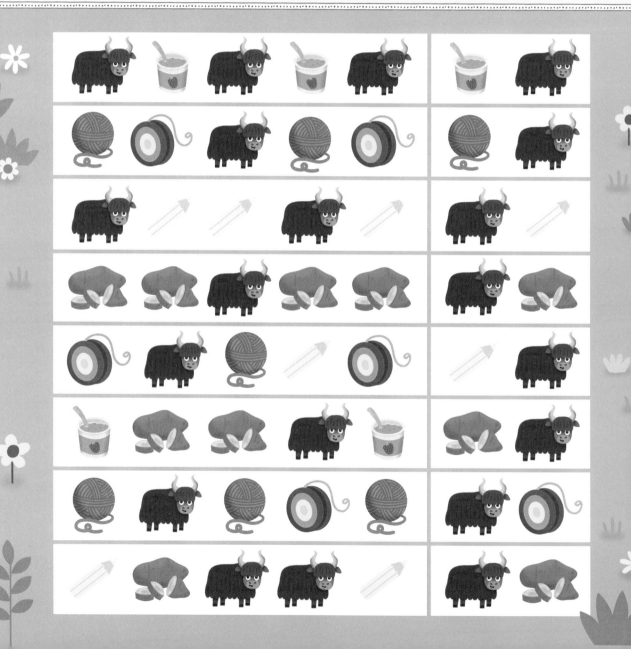

# Zany Zebra

Trace and write.

Zebra _____

Trace the Z words and match to the correct picture.

zigzag

zucchini

zipper

zoo

zero

# Monkey Maze

The monkey is craving a snack. Follow the alphabet from A to Z. Help the hungry monkey collect each banana.

**Start**

| a | b | c | z | k | v | z |
|---|---|---|---|---|---|---|
| z | y | d | w | q | w | p |
| r | v | e | f | g | t | r |

| w | y | u | b | w | s | u | h | q | o |
|---|---|---|---|---|---|---|---|---|---|
| g | s | x | c | z | a | i |  | x | c |
| q |  | p | o | n | v | j | y | s | k |
| r | f | z | w | m | l | k | a | c | y |
| s | h | f | d | g | e | d |
| t | u | v | w | x | y | z | **Finish** |
| a | i | b | c | g | k | h |

# Hop to the Rhyme

These joeys are lost! Help them by circling the objects that rhyme with their mamas. Cross out the rest.

# Flamingo Fun

It's time to rhyme! Use the key to color the rhyming words and reveal a bird that is pretty in pink.

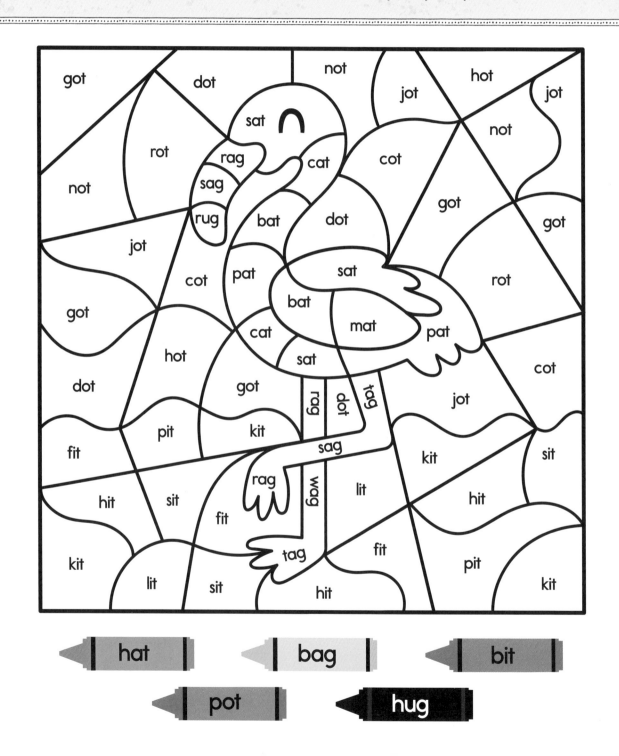

hat  bag  bit

pot  hug

# Chill Out

Help the penguin chill out. Trace the correct
beginning letters for each picture.

# Day at the Zoo

It's a busy day at the zoo! Read the words in the key below. Find the pictures and circle them.

hat    map    net    cub    mop    box    sun    bib    mud

# To the Bamboo

Help the panda find a tasty snack.
Color the path of words with a short vowel.

**Start**

| | | | |
|---|---|---|---|
| hat | lake | nail | fire |
| leg | pig | hot | bug |
| feet | bike | note | cap |
| pole | roof | bee | red |
| fly | mule | tape | mop |

**Finish**

# Playtime

Read the words in the pattern.
Circle what comes next.

| cake | mail | cake | mail | | cake | mail |
| feet | seal | seal | feet | | feet | seal |
| bike | bike | kite | bike | | bike | kite |
| bone | rose | goal | bone | | rose | goal |
| tube | flute | tube | flute | | flute | tube |

# Bubble Blends

Match each bubble to the fish with
the correct ending letters.

MORE READING SKILLS

# A Colorful Surprise

Use the key to color the spaces and reveal a picture.

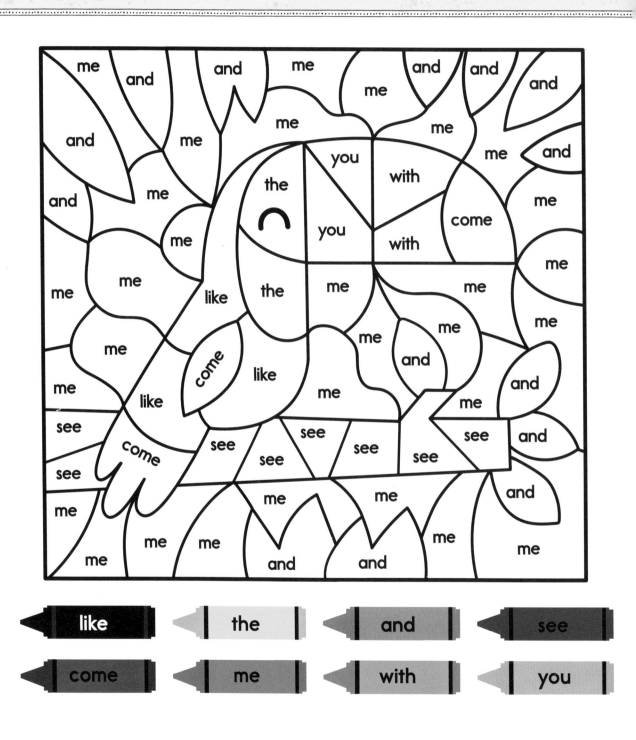

# Out of Sight

Read and trace each sight word.
Find and circle them in the tiger habitat.

what  are  now  find  this

for  said  good  down  look

# Zoom Through the Zoo

Find the zoo's exit by following the path of animal words. Write the animals on the lines.

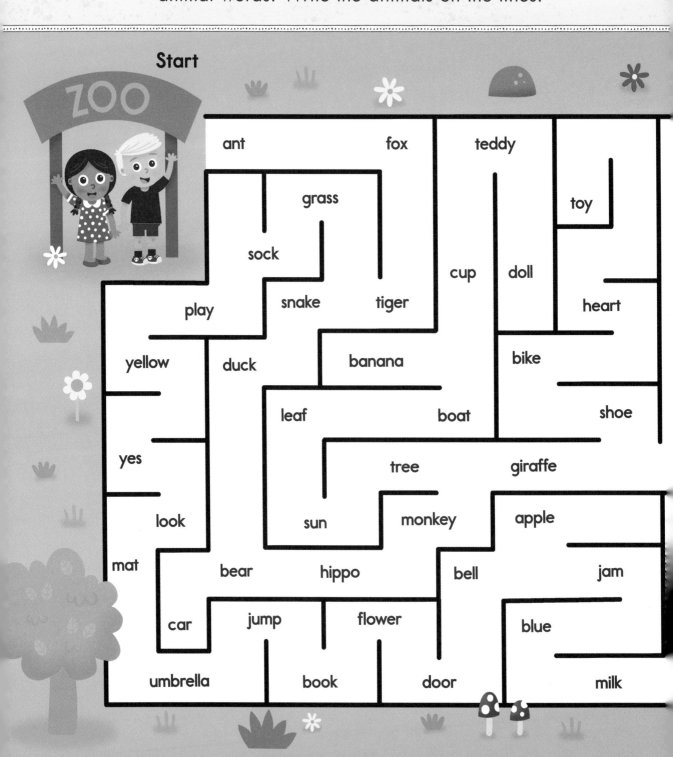

**Start**

ZOO

ant          fox          teddy

grass                          toy

sock                cup    doll

play    snake    tiger              heart

yellow    duck    banana         bike

leaf              boat              shoe

yes                tree        giraffe

look    sun    monkey    apple

mat    bear    hippo    bell    jam

car    jump    flower    blue

umbrella    book    door    milk

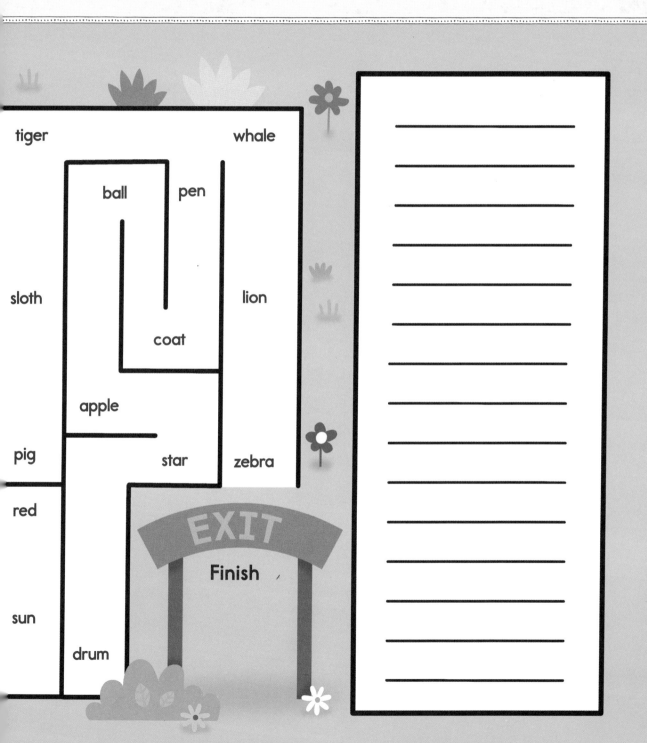

tiger

whale

ball

pen

sloth

lion

coat

apple

pig

star

zebra

red

EXIT

Finish

sun

drum

# Nesting Numbers

Trace the numbers. Draw the correct
number of eggs in each quail nest.

# Who Can Roar?

Use the key to color the picture and see
which animal can roar the loudest!

# Underwater Counting

Splish splash! Count the animals in the aquarium.
Trace the correct number for each group.

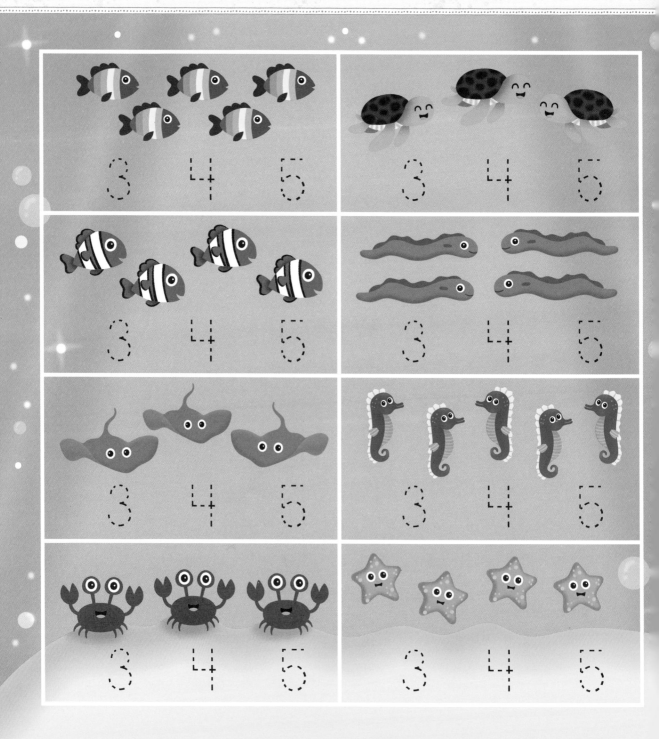

# Peacock Pals

Draw lines to help each peacock find a pal
with the same number of tail feathers.

# Yikes, Stripes!

Trace the numbers. Draw that number of stripes on each zebra.

# Count the Critters

Help the zookeepers count. Circle the correct number of animals in each row.

| 8 | |
| 6 | |
| 7 | |
| 6 | |
| 8 | |
| 7 | |
| 6 | |
| 8 | |

# Tentacle Time

The jellyfish need some tentacles. Trace the numbers.
Draw that number of tentacles.

# Hide-and-Seek

The playful otters love to hide things.
Find and circle numbers 9, 10, and 11.

# Sleepy Sloth

Follow the path to the tree that correctly counts from 0 to 11 so the sloth can catch some zzz's.

# Spot the Spots

Trace the numbers. Match the numbers to the cheetahs with the same number of spots.

# Whooo Do You See?

Use the key to color the picture.
See who is awake at night!

| 13 | 12 | 13 | 13 | 13 | 13 | 13 | 13 | 12 | 13 |
|----|----|----|----|----|----|----|----|----|----|
| 13 | 12 | 12 | 12 | 12 | 12 | 12 | 12 | 12 | 13 |
| 13 | 12 | 11 | 11 | 12 | 12 | 11 | 11 | 11 | 13 |
| 13 | 11 | 10 | 11 | 12 | 12 | 11 | 10 | 11 | 13 |
| 12 | 11 | 11 | 11 | 12 | 12 | 11 | 11 | 11 | 12 |
| 12 | 12 | 12 | 14 | 14 | 14 | 14 | 12 | 12 | 12 |
| 12 | 12 | 12 | 12 | 14 | 14 | 12 | 12 | 12 | 12 |
| 12 | 12 | 12 | 12 | 12 | 12 | 12 | 12 | 12 | 12 |
| 13 | 12 | 12 | 12 | 12 | 12 | 12 | 12 | 12 | 13 |
| 13 | 13 | 12 | 12 | 12 | 12 | 12 | 12 | 13 | 13 |
| 13 | 13 | 13 | 12 | 12 | 12 | 12 | 13 | 13 | 13 |
| 13 | 14 | 14 | 14 | 13 | 13 | 14 | 14 | 14 | 13 |

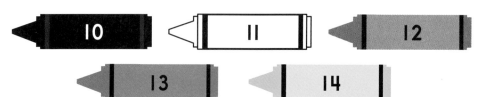

# Pass the Peanuts

Help the elephants get to their favorite snack.
Write what number comes next in each pattern.

15  16  15  16  15  ☐

17  16  15  17  16  ☐

15  15  16  15  15  ☐

16  17  17  16  17  ☐

15  16  17  15  16  ☐

# Fox Trot

Help the fox cross the river. Follow the path of 15, 16, and 17 over the stones.

# Gobbling Giraffe

Crunch, munch! Count the number of leaves on each branch. Circle the correct number.

# River Horse

Use the key to color the picture.
Discover who is nicknamed the "river horse"!

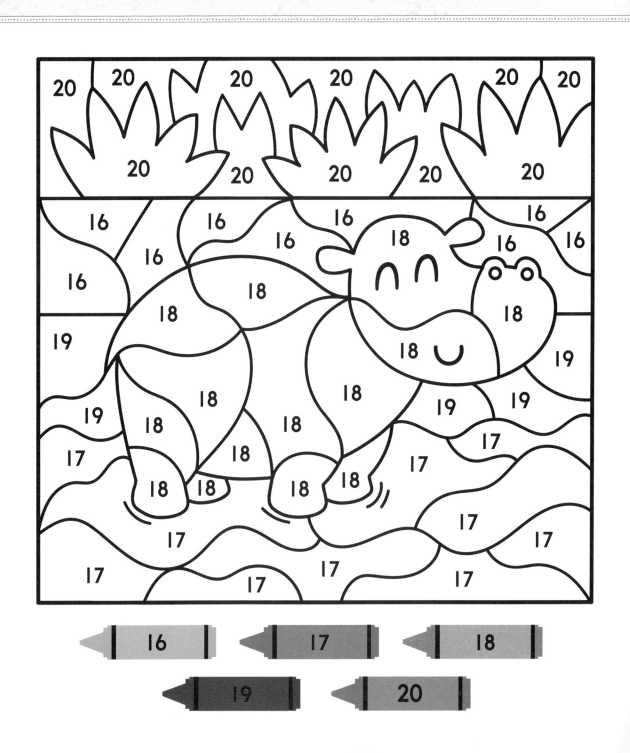

# Connect the Anteater

Connect the dots from 1 to 20 to complete the giant anteater.

# Go Go Gorilla

The gorilla is swinging through the trees!
Follow the path that counts by 2s.

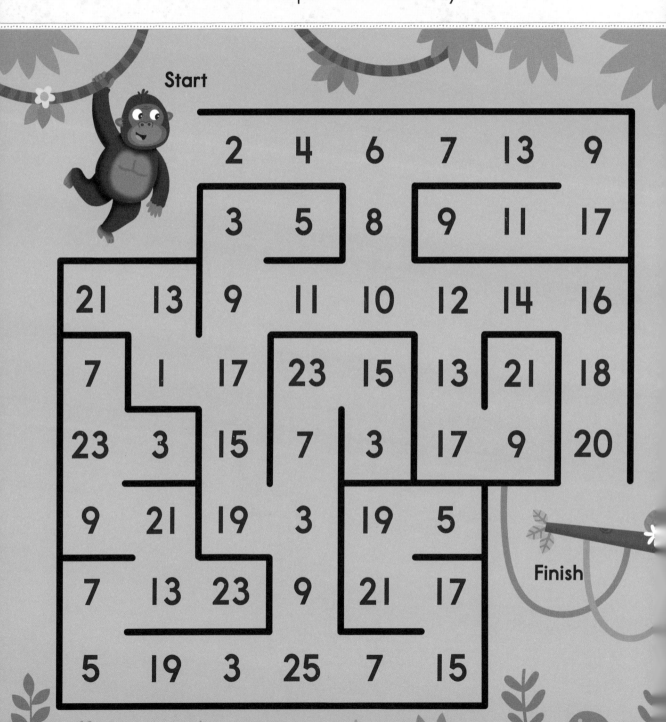

Start

Finish

# High Five

Who flies high in the sky? Count by 5s to connect the dots to find out.

# Interesting Impalas

The impalas are roaming in groups of 10.
Trace or fill in the numbers.

10

____

30

____

50

____

70

____

90

____

# Skip Counting Snakes

What is each snake counting by?
Use the key to color them as they slither by.

10  20  30  40  50  60  70

2  4  6  8  10  12  14

5  10  15  20  25  30  35

10  12  14  16  18  20  22

30  40  50  60  70  80  90

15  20  25  30  35  40  45

2s        5s        10s

# Raccoon Hunt

Help the raccoons find and circle the missing numbers.
Write them in the correct spot on the chart.

| 1 | 2 | 3 | 4 | 5 | | 7 | 8 | 9 | 10 |
|---|---|---|---|---|---|---|---|---|---|
| 11 | | 13 | 14 | 15 | 16 | 17 | 18 | 19 | 20 |
| 21 | 22 | 23 | | 25 | 26 | 27 | 28 | 29 | 30 |
| 31 | 32 | 33 | 34 | 35 | | 37 | 38 | 39 | 40 |
| 41 | 42 | 43 | | 45 | 46 | 47 | 48 | 49 | 50 |
| 51 | | 53 | 54 | | 56 | 57 | 58 | 59 | 60 |
| 61 | 62 | 63 | 64 | 65 | 66 | 67 | | 69 | |
| 71 | 72 | 73 | 74 | 75 | 76 | 77 | 78 | 79 | 80 |
| 81 | 82 | | 84 | 85 | 86 | | 88 | 89 | 90 |
| | 92 | 93 | 94 | 95 | 96 | 97 | 98 | 99 | |

# Match the Mammals

Count each group of animals. Draw a line to another group with the same amount.

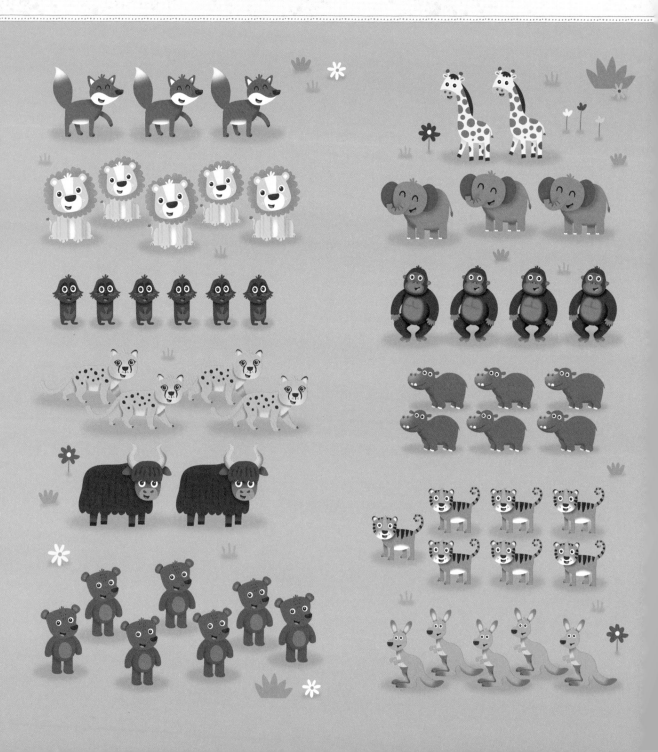

# Up, Down, All Around

Animals are everywhere! Use the key to color animals that fly, swim, or stay on land.

fly | swim | land

# Meerkat Munchies

Count the insects for the meerkats to munch.
Write how many you find.

How many?  ___   ___   ___   ___

Circle which has more:

Circle which has less:

# Two by Two

Count and write the number of animals.
Circle all the pairs and color even or odd.

# Crocodile Smile

Draw teeth on the crocodiles on the right to
make each number sentence true.

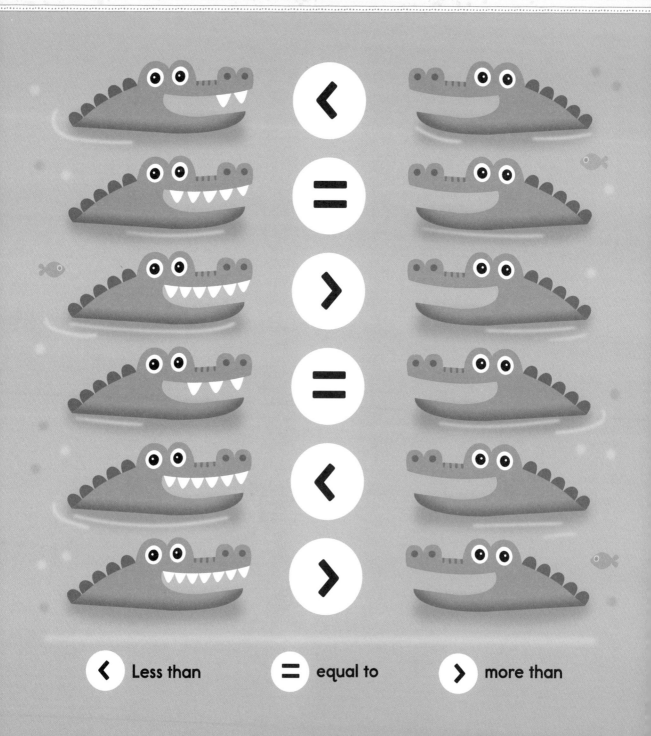

< Less than     = equal to     > more than

# Life on the Savanna

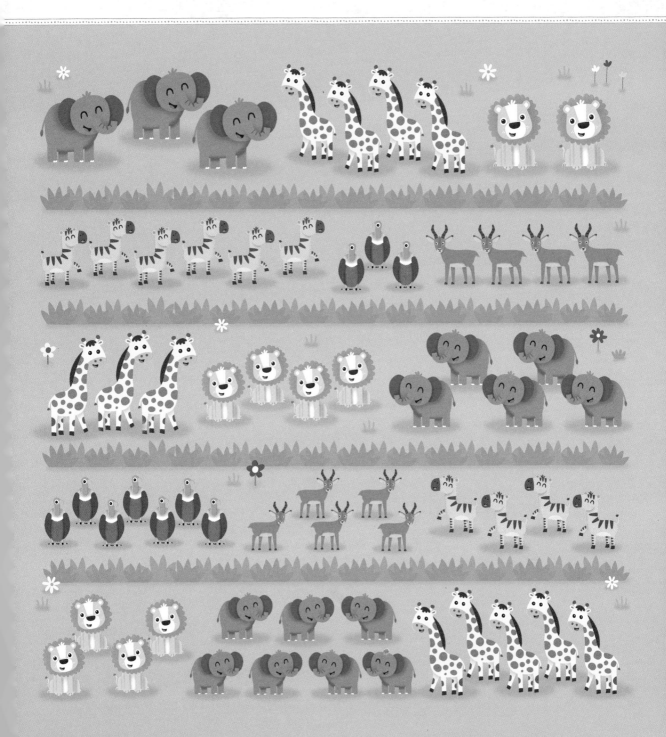

On each row, circle the largest animal herd.
Cross out the smallest group.

# Ant Addition

Add up the ants marching into the anthills.
Trace each correct answer.

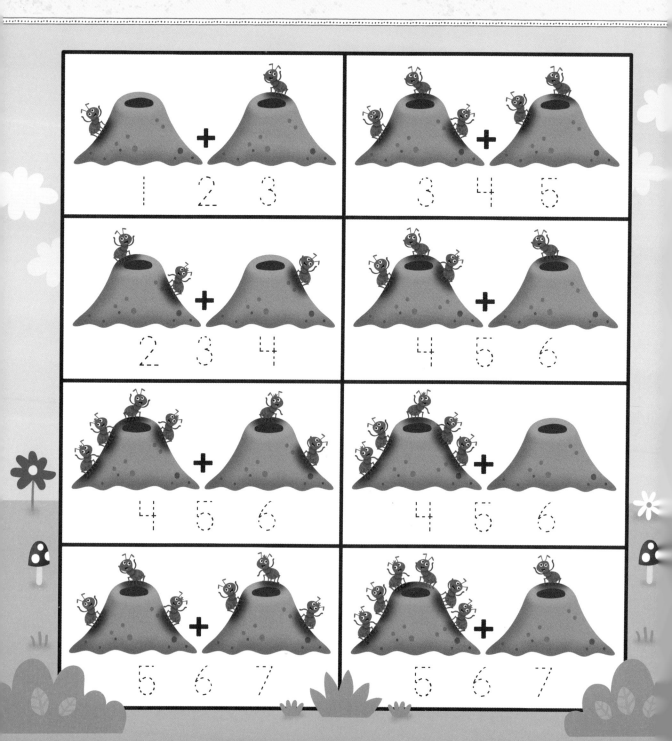

# Banana Bash

Draw more bananas to make 10 for each monkey.
Finish the addition sentence.

$5 + \underline{\phantom{00}} = 10$

$3 + \underline{\phantom{00}} = 10$

$8 + \underline{\phantom{00}} = 10$

$6 + \underline{\phantom{00}} = 10$

$7 + \underline{\phantom{00}} = 10$

$4 + \underline{\phantom{00}} = 10$

$9 + \underline{\phantom{00}} = 10$

$2 + \underline{\phantom{00}} = 10$

# Spider Sums

Add the spiders. Draw a line to help them find their matching webs.

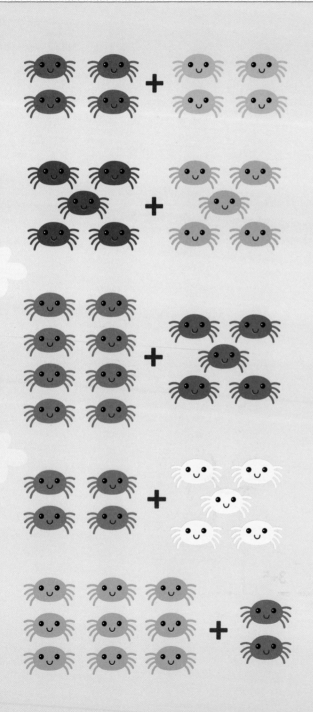

# Unicorn of the Sea

Solve the problems. Use the key to color the picture and reveal the magical swimmer.

| 5 | 6 | 7 | 8 |

# Down the River

Solve the problems. Color a path through
the 5s to help the otter down the river.

| | | | |
|---|---|---|---|
| 10<br>−5 | 9<br>−3 | 6<br>−2 | 7<br>−5 |
| 8<br>−3 | 15<br>−10 | 6<br>−3 | 5<br>−5 |
| 10<br>−2 | 11<br>−6 | 9<br>−2 | 4<br>−1 |
| 11<br>−8 | 10<br>−5 | 12<br>−7 | 6<br>−1 |
| 13<br>−9 | 7<br>−3 | 9<br>−6 | 9<br>−4 |

# Fish Frenzy

The bear is gobbling up the fish! Cross out the fish that are subtracted and write the answer.

3 - 1 = ___

2 - 1 = ___

3 - 2 = ___

4 - 1 = ___

5 - 3 = ___

6 - 4 = ___

5 - 1 = ___

3 - 3 = ___

# To the Turtle Eggs!

Solve the subtraction problems. Color the correct path to guide the turtle to its babies.

Start

| 10-3 | 7 | 10-7 | 3 | 10-5 |
| 6 | | 2 | | 5 |
| 10-2 | 1 | 10-6 | 9 | 10-1 |
| 7 | | 4 | | 2 |
| 10-4 | 2 | 10-8 | 3 | 10-9 |
| 6 | | 7 | | 4 |
| 10-5 | 5 | 10-3 | 7 | Finish |

# Cub Cuties

Help each tiger find their cub. Solve the subtraction problems and draw a line to match.

9-2

8-2

5-3

4-1

7-3

6-1

# Jumbo Fun

Solve each subtraction problem. Then connect the dots to see the largest land animal!

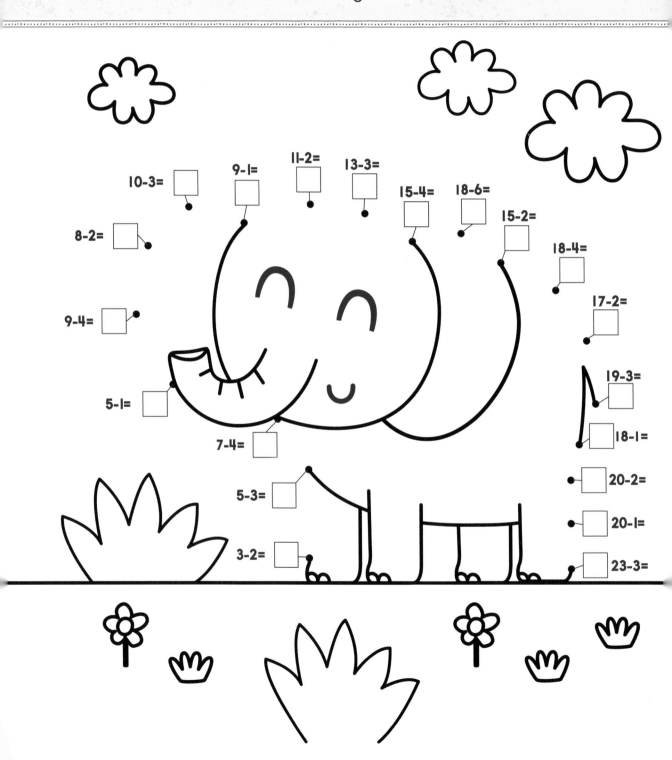

10-3= ☐

9-1= ☐

11-2= ☐

13-3= ☐

15-4= ☐

18-6= ☐

15-2= ☐

18-4= ☐

8-2= ☐

17-2= ☐

9-4= ☐

19-3= ☐

5-1= ☐

18-1= ☐

7-4= ☐

20-2= ☐

5-3= ☐

20-1= ☐

3-2= ☐

23-3= ☐

# Snake Subtraction

Use the key to color the picture to ssssee who is in the tree.

# ANSWER KEY

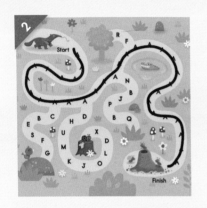

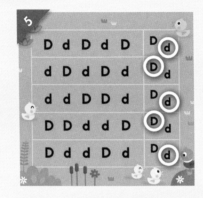

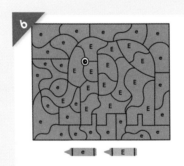

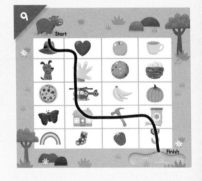

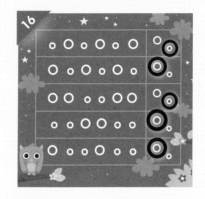

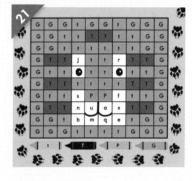

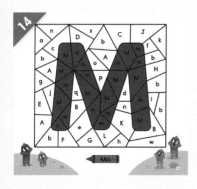

**23**

How many did you find? **12**

**27**

zigzag
zucchini
zipper
zoo
zero

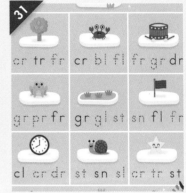

**31**

| cr tr fr | cr bl fl | fr gr dr |
| gr pr fr | gr gl st | sn fl fr |
| cl cr dr | st sn sl | cr tr st |

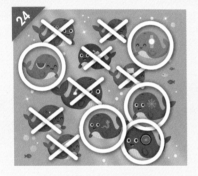

**24**

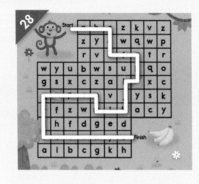

**28**

Start

| | z | k | v | z |
| z y | | w | q | w | p |
| r | v | | | | t | q |
| w | y | u | b | w | s | u | | o |
| g | s | x | c | z | a | | x | c |
| | | | | v | y | s | k |
| f | z | w | | | | a | c | y |
| h | f | d | g | e | d | |

Finish

a i b c g k h

**32**

ZOO

**25**

| x | | w | | W | | y |
| x | | | W | | | W |

**29**

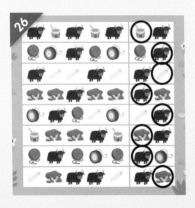

**26**

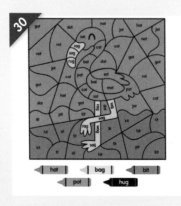

**30**

hat | bag | bit
pot | hug

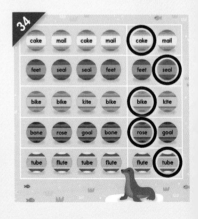

**33**

Start

| hat | lake | nail | fire |
| leg | pig | hot | bug |
| feet | bike | note | cap |
| pole | roof | bee | red |
| fly | mule | tape | mop |

Finish

**34**

| cake | mail | cake | mail | cake | mail |
| feet | seal | seal | feet | feet | seal |
| bike | bike | kite | bike | bike | kite |
| bone | rose | goal | bone | rose | goal |
| tube | flute | tube | flute | flute | tube |

**35**

**39**

**42**

**36**

**40**

**43**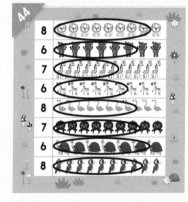

**37**

what   are   now   find   this
for   said   good   down   look

**41**

**44**

**38**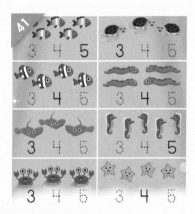

ant
fox
tiger
snake
duck
bear
hippo
monkey
giraffe
pig
sloth
tiger
whale
lion
zebra

**45**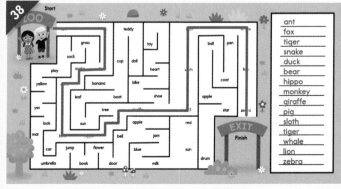

50

| 15 | 16 | 15 | 16 | 15 | **16** |
| 17 | 16 | 15 | 17 | 16 | **15** |
| 15 | 15 | 16 | 15 | 15 | **16** |
| 16 | 17 | 17 | 16 | 17 | **17** |
| 15 | 16 | 17 | 15 | 16 | **17** |

54

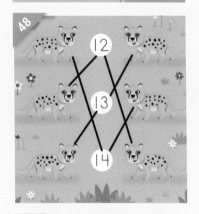

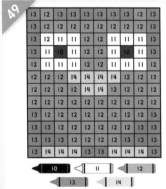

**58**

10 20 30 40 50 60 70

2 4 6 8 10 12 14

5 10 15 20 25 30 35

10 12 14 16 18 20 22

30 40 50 60 70 80 90

15 20 25 30 35 40 45

2s   5s   10s

**62**

How many?  3   8   7   5

Circle which has more:

Circle which has less:

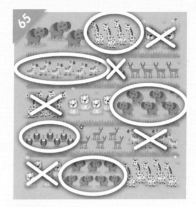

**65**

**59**

| 1 | 2 | 3 | 4 | 5 | 6 | 7 | 8 | 9 | 10 |
|---|---|---|---|---|---|---|---|---|----|
| 11 | 12 | 13 | 14 | 15 | 16 | 17 | 18 | 19 | 20 |
| 21 | 22 | 23 | 24 | 25 | 26 | 27 | 28 | 29 | 30 |
| 31 | 32 | 33 | 34 | 35 | 36 | 37 | 38 | 39 | 40 |
| 41 | 42 | 43 | 44 | 45 | 46 | 47 | 48 | 49 | 50 |
| 51 | 52 | 53 | 54 | 55 | 56 | 57 | 58 | 59 | 60 |
| 61 | 62 | 63 | 64 | 65 | 66 | 67 | 68 | 69 | 70 |
| 71 | 72 | 73 | 74 | 75 | 76 | 77 | 78 | 79 | 80 |
| 81 | 82 | 83 | 84 | 85 | 86 | 87 | 88 | 89 | 90 |
| 91 | 92 | 93 | 94 | 95 | 96 | 97 | 98 | 99 | 100 |

**66**

| + | 1 2 3 | + | 3 4 5 |
|---|-------|---|-------|
| + | 2 3 4 | + | 4 5 6 |
| + | 4 5 6 | | 4 5 6 |
| + | 5 6 7 | + | 5 6 7 |

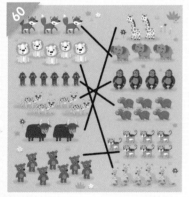

**60**

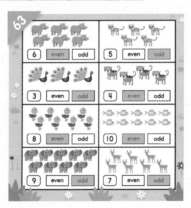

**63**

| 6 | even | odd | 5 | even | odd |
| 3 | even | odd | 4 | even | odd |
| 8 | even | odd | 10 | even | odd |
| 9 | even | odd | 7 | even | odd |

**67**

5+ _5_ =10     3+ _7_ =10

8+ _2_ =10     6+ _4_ =10

7+ _3_ =10     4+ _6_ =10

9+ _1_ =10     2+ _8_ =10

**61**

**64**

<     or more

=

>     or fewer

=

<     or more

>     or fewer

**68**

10 12 8 11 9 13

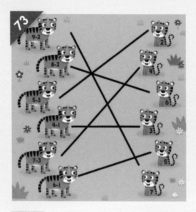

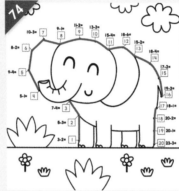

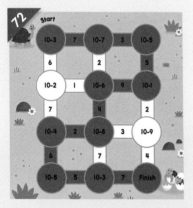

# ABOUT THE AUTHOR

**Lauren Thompson** earned her BS in interdisciplinary studies with an early childhood certification from Texas A&M University-Commerce. She taught third grade at a public school in Texas before moving overseas with her family. She spent almost 10 years in the Middle East partnering with nonprofit organizations while homeschooling her five children. She started Mrs. Thompson's Treasures (MrsThompsonsTreasures.com) as a way to share fun and engaging resources for elementary school teachers and parents. Lauren lives with her family in Texas and loves to visit new places, read, and drink lots of coffee.

# ABOUT THE ILLUSTRATOR

**Jennie Bradley** has a degree in graphic communication and has freelanced from her home studio since 2011, fueled by tea and a constant stream of music! When Jennie isn't being nearly eaten by a lion in Botswana, getting a black eye white water rafting down the Zambezi River, or being chased by an angry warthog (all true stories), she can be found snuggled up with her superstar son, watching *Labyrinth*, celebrating Arsenal wins, visiting the theater, or dreaming about touring Australia.